HEY THERE, HUNGRY COLLEGE STUDENT!

We know you're not exactly the experienced chef, and we totally get it... **you're on a budget!**

But guess what? That doesn't mean you have to live off instant noodles and takeout!

This cookbook is **your new dorm bestie**, packed with recipes that are **cheap**, **healthy**, and **ridiculously easy** to whip up.

WHAT YOU'LL FIND IN THIS AMAZING COOKBOOK!

Cheap Recipes

Save your money for coffee and fun! These recipes are budget-friendly and still taste amazing.

Easy to Cook!

No fancy tools, no stress. If you can use a microwave or a pan, you're good to go!

Fullfilling Meals

No more staying hungry. These recipes are hearty and will keep you full!

No Oven, No Problem!

Some recipes call for an oven, but don't worry. Ff you don't have one, a regular pan or microwave will get the job done too!

FIND YOUR FAVORITE RECIPES BY INGREDIENT OR CATEGORY

Chicken
p17, 20, 27, 28, 39, 51, 59, 70, 81

Egg
6, 10, 29, 33, 40, 46, 57, 66, 76

Rice
4, 26, 28, 32, 39, 43, 45, 50, 67, 80

Pasta
12, 29, 33, 40, 46, 49, 53, 78, 83

Cheese
8, 12, 13, 16, 33, 46, 52, 62, 75

Vegetables
4, 9, 24, 28, 30, 32, 36, 42, 47, 49, 64,

Bread
5, 8, 25, 30, 44, 66

Potatoes
16, 22, 27, 38, 50, 63, 77

RICE AND BEAN BOWL

1 PERSON

$1.5 / PERSON

INGREDIENTS

- 1 cup rice
- 1 can black or kidney beans
- ½ cup salsa
- ¼ cup shredded cheese
- 1 lime

HOW TO COOK

- Cook rice according to package instructions.
- Heat beans in a saucepan until warm.
- In a bowl, combine rice, beans, salsa, and cheese.
- Squeeze lime juice over the top before serving.

PEANUT BUTTER BANANA WRAP

1 PERSON

$1 / PERSON

INGREDIENTS

- 1 tortilla
- 2 tablespoons peanut butter
- 1 banana
- 1 teaspoon honey
- A pinch of cinnamon

HOW TO COOK

- Spread peanut butter evenly over the tortilla.
- Place the peeled banana on one edge of the tortilla.
- Drizzle honey over the banana and sprinkle with cinnamon.
- Roll up the tortilla around the banana and slice in half. Squeeze lime juice over the top before serving.

5

EGG FRIED RICE

1 PERSON

$1.25 / PERSON

INGREDIENTS

- 1 cup cooked rice (preferably day-old)
- 2 eggs
- 1 cup frozen mixed vegetables
- 2 tablespoons soy sauce
- 1 tablespoon sesame oil (optional)

HOW TO COOK

- In a pan, heat sesame oil over medium heat.
- Add frozen vegetables and sauté until tender.
- Push vegetables to the side and scramble eggs in the same pan.
- Add rice and soy sauce, mixing everything together until heated through.

INSTANT RAMEN UPGRADE

1 PERSON

$1 / PERSON

INGREDIENTS

- 1 pack instant ramen
- 1 egg
- 1 cup fresh spinach or bok choy
- 1 tablespoon soy sauce
- ½ teaspoon chili flakes

HOW TO COOK

- Cook ramen noodles according to package instructions, adding the seasoning packet.
- During the last minute of cooking, add spinach or bok choy.
- Crack an egg into the boiling broth and let it poach for 2-3 minutes.
- Serve hot, seasoned with soy sauce and chili flakes.

GRILLED CHEESE SANDWICH

 1 PERSON

 $1.5 / PERSON

INGREDIENTS

- 2 slices bread
- 2 tablespoons butter
- 2 slices cheese
- 1 tomato (optional)
- A pinch of garlic powder

HOW TO COOK

- Butter one side of each bread slice.
- Place one slice, butter-side down, in a heated pan.
- Add cheese slices and tomato if using, then top with the second bread slice, butter-side up.
- Cook until golden brown on both sides, sprinkling with garlic powder before serving.

VEGETABLE STIR-FRY

1 PERSON

$1.8 / PERSON

INGREDIENTS

- 2 cups frozen mixed vegetables
- 2 tablespoons soy sauce
- 1 clove garlic, minced
- 1 teaspoon ginger (fresh or powdered)
- 1 cup cooked rice or noodles

HOW TO COOK

- In a pan, heat oil over medium heat.
- Add garlic and ginger, sautéing until fragrant.
- Add frozen vegetables and cook until tender.
- Stir in soy sauce and serve over rice or noodles.

BREAKFAST-FOR-DINNER SCRAMBLE

1 PERSON

$1.5 / PERSON

INGREDIENTS

- 2 eggs
- 1 potato, diced
- ½ onion, chopped
- ½ bell pepper, chopped
- ¼ cup shredded cheese

HOW TO COOK

- In a pan, cook diced potato until tender.
- Add onion and bell pepper, sautéing until soft.
- Whisk eggs and pour into the pan, scrambling with the vegetables.
- Once cooked, sprinkle with cheese and serve.

10

TUNA MELT

1 PERSON

$2 / PERSON

INGREDIENTS

- 2 slices bread
- 1 can tuna, drained
- 2 tablespoons mayonnaise
- 2 slices cheese
- ¼ onion, finely chopped (optional)

HOW TO COOK

- Mix tuna with mayonnaise and onion if using.
- Spread the mixture on one slice of bread, top with cheese, and cover with the second slice.
- Grill in a pan until bread is toasted and cheese is melted.

PASTA WITH TOMATO SAUCE

2 PEOPLE

$1.25 / PERSON

INGREDIENTS

- 2 cups pasta
- 1 cup canned tomato sauce
- 1 clove garlic, minced
- 1 tablespoon olive oil
- 1 teaspoon dried basil

HOW TO COOK

- Cook pasta according to package instructions.
- In a pan, heat olive oil and sauté garlic until fragrant.
- Add tomato sauce and basil, simmering for 5 minutes.
- Toss cooked pasta in the sauce and serve.

QUESADILLA

2 PEOPLE

$1.75 / PERSON

INGREDIENTS

- 2 tortillas
- 1 cup shredded cheese
- ½ cup canned beans, drained
- ¼ cup salsa
- 2 tablespoons sour cream (optional)

HOW TO COOK

- On one tortilla, layer cheese and beans.
- Top with the second tortilla.
- Cook in a pan over medium heat until both sides are golden and cheese is melted.
- Serve with salsa and sour cream.

MICROWAVE CHILI MAC

 1 PERSON

 $1.5 / PERSON

INGREDIENTS

- 1 cup cooked pasta
- ½ cup canned chili
- ¼ cup shredded cheese
- 1 tsp hot sauce (optional)

HOW TO COOK

- Combine pasta and chili in a microwave-safe bowl.
- Microwave for 2 minutes.
- Stir, top with shredded cheese, and microwave for another 30 seconds until the cheese melts.
- Drizzle hot sauce if desired.

MICROWAVE BURRITO BOWL

1 PERSON

$1.75 / PERSON

INGREDIENTS

- 1 cup cooked rice
- ½ cup black beans
- ½ cup salsa
- ¼ cup shredded cheese
- 2 tbsp sour cream

HOW TO COOK

- Combine rice, beans, and salsa in a microwave-safe bowl.
- Microwave for 2 minutes.
- Stir, top with cheese, and microwave for another 30 seconds.
- Add sour cream and mix before serving.

MICROWAVE MASHED POTATOES

1 PERSON

$1.5 / PERSON

INGREDIENTS

- 2 potatoes
- ¼ cup milk
- ¼ cup shredded cheese
- 2 tbsp sour cream
- Bacon bits or green onion (optional)

HOW TO COOK

- Dice potatoes and place in a microwave-safe bowl with water. Cover with plastic wrap.
- Microwave for 5-7 minutes or until soft.
- Drain water and mash potatoes with milk, cheese, and sour cream.
- Top with bacon bits or green onion if desired.

MICROWAVE CHICKEN QUESADILLA

1 PERSON

$2 / PERSON

INGREDIENTS

- 2 tortillas
- ½ cup shredded chicken (rotisserie or canned)
- ½ cup shredded cheese
- 2 tbsp salsa
- Sour cream (optional)

HOW TO COOK

- Place chicken and cheese on one tortilla.
- Top with the second tortilla.
- Microwave for 1-2 minutes until the cheese is melted.
- Slice and serve with salsa and sour cream.

MICROWAVE SHEPHERD'S PIE

1 PERSON

$1.8 / PERSON

INGREDIENTS

- 1 cup frozen mixed vegetables
- ½ cup cooked ground beef or turkey
- 1 cup mashed potatoes
- 2 tbsp gravy

HOW TO COOK

- Layer vegetables, meat, and gravy in a microwave-safe bowl.
- Top with mashed potatoes.
- Microwave for 3-4 minutes until heated through.

MICROWAVE RAMEN STIR-FRY

1 PERSON

$1.25 / PERSON

INGREDIENTS

- 1 pack instant ramen
- 1 egg
- ½ cup frozen veggies
- 2 tbsp soy sauce
- 1 tsp sesame oil (optional)

HOW TO COOK

- Cook ramen in less water than usual in the microwave.
- Stir in the egg and frozen veggies.
- Microwave for another 1-2 minutes.
- Add soy sauce and sesame oil, then stir.

MICROWAVE BBQ CHICKEN RICE BOWL

1 PERSON

$1.75 / PERSON

INGREDIENTS

- 1 cup cooked rice
- ½ cup shredded chicken
- ¼ cup BBQ sauce
- 2 tbsp sour cream
- Green onion (optional)

HOW TO COOK

- Combine rice and chicken in a microwave-safe bowl.
- Add BBQ sauce and microwave for 2 minutes.
- Top with sour cream and green onion before serving.

MICROWAVE TUNA CASSEROLE

1 PERSON

$1.5 / PERSON

INGREDIENTS

- 1 cup cooked pasta
- ½ cup canned tuna
- ¼ cup shredded cheese
- 2 tbsp mayonnaise
- 2 tbsp peas (optional)

HOW TO COOK

- Mix pasta, tuna, mayo, and peas in a microwave-safe bowl.
- Microwave for 2 minutes.
- Sprinkle cheese on top and microwave for another 30 seconds.

MICROWAVE SWEET POTATO BOWL

1 PERSON

$1.25 / PERSON

INGREDIENTS

- 1 sweet potato
- ¼ cup black beans
- 2 tbsp shredded cheese
- 2 tbsp salsa
- 1 tsp hot sauce (optional)

HOW TO COOK

- Poke holes in the sweet potato and microwave for 5-7 minutes.
- Slice open and mash lightly.
- Top with beans, cheese, salsa, and hot sauce.

MICROWAVE MEATBALL SUB

1 PERSON

$2.25 / PERSON

INGREDIENTS

- 1 hoagie roll
- 3-4 frozen meatballs
- ¼ cup marinara sauce
- ¼ cup shredded mozzarella
- Garlic powder (optional)t

HOW TO COOK

- Heat meatballs and marinara sauce in a microwave-safe bowl for 2-3 minutes.
- Place meatballs and sauce in the hoagie roll.
- Top with mozzarella and sprinkle garlic powder.
- Microwave for 30 seconds until the cheese melts.

CHICKEN CAESAR WRAP

1 PERSON

$2.5 / PERSON

INGREDIENTS

- Tortilla
- Shredded chicken
- Lettuce
- Caesar dressing
- Parmesan cheese

HOW TO COOK

- Layer lettuce, chicken, and parmesan on a tortilla.
- Drizzle Caesar dressing and roll into a wrap.

STIR-FRIED UDON WITH VEGETABLES

1 PERSON

$2.5 / PERSON

INGREDIENTS

- Udon noodles
- Bell peppers
- Carrots
- Soy sauce
- Sesame oil.

HOW TO COOK

- Boil udon noodles and set aside.
- Stir-fry sliced bell peppers and carrots in sesame oil.
- Add noodles, soy sauce, and toss until combined.

LENTIL AND RICE BOWL

1 PERSON

$1.75 / PERSON

INGREDIENTS

- 1 cup lentils
- 1 cup rice
- 1 cup spinach
- 2 tbsp olive oil
- 2 cloves garlic

HOW TO COOK

- Boil lentils and rice together in a pot until tender.
- Sauté spinach with olive oil and minced garlic in a pan until wilted.
- Serve the spinach mixture over the cooked lentils and rice.

BAKED CHICKEN DRUMSTICKS WITH SWEET POTATOES

1 PERSON

$2.5 / PERSON

INGREDIENTS

- 2 chicken drumsticks
- 2 sweet potatoes (halved)
- 2 tbsp olive oil
- 1 tsp paprika
- ½ tsp salt

HOW TO COOK

- Rub the chicken drumsticks with olive oil, paprika, and salt.
- Place the drumsticks and halved sweet potatoes on a baking sheet.
- Roast at 400°F (200°C) for 25–30 minutes or until fully cooked.

SHRIMP AND VEGETABLE STIR-FRY

1 PERSON

$3 / PERSON

INGREDIENTS

- 1 cup shrimp (peeled and deveined)
- 1 cup broccoli florets
- ½ cup carrots (sliced)
- 2 tbsp soy sauce
- 1 tsp grated ginger

HOW TO COOK

- Heat a pan and stir-fry shrimp until they turn pink.
- Add broccoli and carrots, cooking until tender.
- Toss with soy sauce and grated ginger before serving.

VEGETABLE AND EGG FRIED NOODLES

1 PERSON

$2.25 / PERSON

INGREDIENTS

- 1 cup egg noodles (cooked)
- 2 eggs
- 1 cup cabbage (shredded)
- 2 tbsp soy sauce
- 1 tsp sesame oil

HOW TO COOK

- Boil the egg noodles and set aside.
- Heat sesame oil in a pan and scramble the eggs.
- Add cabbage and stir-fry for 2 minutes. Toss in the cooked noodles and soy sauce until well combined.

TURKEY AND AVOCADO SANDWICH

1 PERSON

$2.5 / PERSON

INGREDIENTS

- 2 slices of bread
- 3 slices of turkey
- ½ avocado (sliced)
- 2 lettuce leaves
- 1 tbsp mayonnaise

HOW TO COOK

- Toast the bread slices and spread mayonnaise on one side.
- Layer the turkey slices, avocado, and lettuce between the bread slices.

OVEN-BAKED ZUCCHINI BOATS

1 PERSON

$2.75 / PERSON

INGREDIENTS

- 2 zucchinis (halved lengthwise)
- ½ cup ground turkey or beef
- ½ cup marinara sauce
- ½ cup shredded cheese
- 2 tbsp breadcrumbs

HOW TO COOK

- Hollow out the zucchini halves and fill them with cooked ground turkey mixed with marinara sauce.
- Sprinkle shredded cheese and breadcrumbs on top.
- Bake at 375ºF (190ºC) for 20 minutes.

COUSCOUS WITH ROASTED VEGETABLES

1 PERSON

$2.5 / PERSON

INGREDIENTS

- 1 cup cooked couscous
- 1 zucchini (diced)
- 1 carrot (diced)
- 2 tbsp olive oil
- ½ tsp garlic powder

HOW TO COOK

- Toss diced zucchini and carrots with olive oil and garlic powder.
- Roast at 375°F (190°C) for 20 minutes or until tender.
- Mix roasted vegetables with cooked couscous and serve.

EGGPLANT PARMESAN

1 PERSON

$2.75 / PERSON

INGREDIENTS

- 1 large eggplant (sliced)
- ½ cup marinara sauce
- ½ cup breadcrumbs
- ½ cup shredded mozzarella
- ¼ cup grated parmesan

HOW TO COOK

- Slice eggplant and coat in breadcrumbs.
- Layer in a baking dish with marinara sauce and mozzarella.
- Bake at 375°F (190°C) for 25 minutes, topping with parmesan before serving.

CHICKPEA CURRY WITH RICE

2 PEOPLE

$1.75 / PERSON

INGREDIENTS

- 1 cup cooked rice
- ½ cup canned chickpeas
- ½ cup coconut milk
- 1 tsp curry powder
- Salt to taste

HOW TO COOK

- Heat chickpeas with coconut milk and curry powder in a pan until thickened.
- Serve over cooked rice.

BEEF AND BROCCOLI STIR-FRY

2 PEOPLE

$2.5 / PERSON

INGREDIENTS

- ½ lb ground beef or thinly sliced beef
- 1 cup broccoli
- 2 tbsp soy sauce
- 1 tbsp cornstarch (optional)
- 1 tsp sesame oil

HOW TO COOK

- Stir-fry beef until browned.
- Add broccoli and soy sauce; cook until tender.
- Toss with sesame oil and cornstarch slurry if desired for thickening.

SHAKSHUKA

2 PEOPLE

$1.75 / PERSON

INGREDIENTS

- 2 eggs
- ½ cup canned diced tomatoes
- 1 small onion
- 1 tsp paprika
- Olive oil

HOW TO COOK

- Sauté chopped onion in olive oil until translucent.
- Add diced tomatoes and paprika; simmer for 5 minutes.
- Make two small wells in the sauce and crack eggs into them. Cover and cook until eggs are set.

TUNA AND VEGETABLE PASTA

2 PEOPLE

$2 / PERSON

INGREDIENTS

- 1 cup pasta
- ½ cup canned tuna
- 1 cup frozen mixed vegetables
- 2 tbsp olive oil
- Salt and pepper to taste

HOW TO COOK

- Cook pasta and drain.
- Toss pasta with tuna, vegetables, olive oil, salt, and pepper.

BAKED POTATO WITH COTTAGE CHEESE

1 PERSON

$1.5 / PERSON

INGREDIENTS

- 1 large potato
- ½ cup cottage cheese
- Green onions (optional)
- Salt
- Pepper

HOW TO COOK

- Microwave or bake potato until tender.
- Slice open and top with cottage cheese, salt, pepper, and green onions.
- Add a drizzle of olive oil for a creamy texture or chili flakes for a kick.

CHICKEN AND VEGETABLE SOUP

2 PEOPLE

$2.25 / PERSON

INGREDIENTS

- 1 cup shredded chicken (rotisserie or canned)
- 1 cup chicken broth
- ½ cup frozen mixed vegetables
- 1 small potato (optional)
- Salt and pepper

HOW TO COOK

- Heat broth with chicken and vegetables.
- Add diced potato if desired and cook until tender. Season to taste.

SCRAMBLED EGGS WITH SPINACH AND CHEESE

1 PERSON

$1.75 / PERSON

INGREDIENTS

- 2 eggs
- ½ cup fresh spinach
- ¼ cup shredded cheese
- 1 tbsp butter
- Salt and pepper

HOW TO COOK

- Heat butter in a pan, add spinach, and cook until wilted.
- Add whisked eggs and cook while stirring. Top with cheese, salt, and pepper.

GROUND TURKEY LETTUCE WRAPS

2 PEOPLE

$2.5 / PERSON

INGREDIENTS

- ½ lb ground turkey
- Lettuce leaves
- Soy sauce
- Garlic
- Olive oil

HOW TO COOK

- Cook turkey with minced garlic and soy sauce until browned.
- Serve in lettuce leaves as wraps.

CHICKPEA AND SPINACH STEW

2 PEOPLE

$1.75 / PERSON

INGREDIENTS

- 1 cup canned chickpeas
- 1 cup spinach
- ½ cup canned diced tomatoes
- Garlic
- Olive oil

HOW TO COOK

- Heat olive oil in a pan, add garlic, and sauté until fragrant.
- Add chickpeas, spinach, and tomatoes. Simmer for 10 minutes.

SPAGHETTI WITH GARLIC AND OLIVE OIL

2 PEOPLE

$1.75 / PERSON

INGREDIENTS

- 1 cup spaghetti
- 2 tbsp olive oil
- 2 cloves garlic
- Red pepper flakes
- Parmesan cheese

HOW TO COOK

- Cook spaghetti and set aside.
- Heat olive oil in a pan, add minced garlic, and red pepper flakes.
  Toss with spaghetti and top with parmesan.

SLOPPY JOE SANDWICH

2 PEOPLE

$2.25 / PERSON

INGREDIENTS

- ½ lb ground beef or turkey
- ½ cup ketchup
- 1 tbsp mustard
- 2 sandwich buns
- Salt and pepper

HOW TO COOK

- Cook ground meat in a pan until browned.
- Mix ketchup, mustard, salt, and pepper, and stir into the meat.
- Serve on sandwich buns.

BAKED SALMON WITH RICE

1 PERSON

$3.5 / PERSON

INGREDIENTS

- 1 salmon fillet
- 1 cup cooked rice
- 1 tbsp soy sauce
- Lemon juice
- Olive oil

HOW TO COOK

- Drizzle salmon with soy sauce, olive oil, and lemon juice.
- Bake at 375ºF (190ºC) for 12–15 minutes.
- Serve with cooked rice.

VEGGIE AND CHEESE OMELETTE

1 PERSON

$1.5 / PERSON

INGREDIENTS

- 2 eggs
- ½ cup diced vegetables (onion, bell pepper, spinach)
- ¼ cup shredded cheese
- 1 tbsp butter
- Salt and pepper

HOW TO COOK

- Whisk eggs with salt and pepper.
- Sauté veggies in butter until tender, then add eggs.
- Sprinkle cheese on top and cook until set.

QUINOA AND ROASTED VEGETABLES

2 PEOPLE

$2 / PERSON

INGREDIENTS

- 1 cup cooked quinoa
- 1 zucchini, diced
- 1 carrot, diced
- Olive oil
- Garlic powder

HOW TO COOK

- Toss vegetables with olive oil and garlic powder, and roast at 375°F (190°C) for 20 minutes.
- Serve roasted vegetables over cooked quinoa.

TURKEY CHILI

2 PEOPLE

$2.25 / PERSON

INGREDIENTS

- ½ lb ground turkey
- 1 cup canned diced tomatoes
- ½ cup canned beans (black or kidney)
- 1 tsp chili powder
- Salt and pepper

HOW TO COOK

- Cook turkey in a pan until browned.
- Add tomatoes, beans, chili powder, salt, and pepper.
- Simmer for 10–15 minutes.

PASTA PRIMAVERA

2 PEOPLE

$2.25 / PERSON

INGREDIENTS

- 1 cup pasta
- 1 cup mixed vegetables (zucchini, broccoli, carrots)
- Olive oil
- Garlic
- Parmesan cheese

HOW TO COOK

- Cook pasta and drain.
- Sauté vegetables and garlic in olive oil until tender.
- Toss with pasta and sprinkle with parmesan.

GROUND BEEF AND POTATO SKILLET

2 PEOPLE

$2.5 / PERSON

INGREDIENTS

- ½ lb ground beef
- 2 potatoes, diced
- 1 small onion
- Salt and pepper
- Olive oil

HOW TO COOK

- Cook ground beef in a pan until browned. Remove and set aside.
- In the same pan, sauté onions and potatoes in olive oil until tender.
- Add beef back to the pan, season with salt and pepper, and serve.

CHICKEN AND BROCCOLI ALFREDO

2 PEOPLE

$2.5 / PERSON

INGREDIENTS

- 1 cup cooked pasta
- ½ cup cooked chicken (shredded or diced)
- ½ cup broccoli
- ¼ cup alfredo sauce
- Parmesan cheese

HOW TO COOK

- Heat chicken, broccoli, and alfredo sauce together in a pan or microwave.
- Toss with cooked pasta and top with parmesan.

GRILLED CHEESE AND TOMATO SOUP

1 PERSON

$2.5 / PERSON

INGREDIENTS

- 2 slices bread
- 2 slices cheese
- 1 tbsp butter
- 1 cup canned tomato soup
- Milk or water (for soup)

HOW TO COOK

- Butter bread and grill with cheese in a pan until golden.
- Heat tomato soup with milk or water and serve with the sandwich.

PEANUT BUTTER NOODLES

1 PERSON

$2 / PERSON

INGREDIENTS

- 1 cup cooked spaghetti or rice noodles
- 2 tbsp peanut butter
- 1 tbsp soy sauce
- 1 tsp honey
- Chili flakes (optional)

HOW TO COOK

- Mix peanut butter, soy sauce, honey, and chili flakes into a sauce.
- Toss noodles with the sauce and serve.

BLACK BEAN AND CORN SALAD

2 PEOPLE

$2 / PERSON

INGREDIENTS

- 1 cup black beans (canned)
- 1 cup corn (canned or frozen)
- ½ cup diced tomatoes
- 1 tbsp olive oil
- Juice of 1 lime

HOW TO COOK

- Mix black beans, corn, and diced tomatoes in a bowl.
- Drizzle with olive oil and lime juice, then toss to combine.

KOREAN BEEF BOWLS

2 PEOPLE

$2.5 / PERSON

INGREDIENTS

- ½ lb ground beef
- 2 tbsp soy sauce
- 1 tbsp brown sugar
- 1 clove garlic (minced)
- 1 tsp sesame oil

HOW TO COOK

- Cook ground beef in a pan until browned.
- Add soy sauce, brown sugar, garlic, and sesame oil. Stir until combined.
- Serve over cooked rice.

MUSHROOM AND SPINACH RISOTTO

2 PEOPLE

$3 / PERSON

INGREDIENTS

- 1 cup Arborio rice
- 1 cup mushrooms (sliced)
- 1 cup spinach
- 2 cups chicken or vegetable broth
- ¼ cup grated parmesan cheese

HOW TO COOK

- Sauté mushrooms in olive oil, then add rice and toast for 1-2 minutes.
- Gradually add broth, stirring constantly, until rice is creamy and cooked.
- Stir in spinach and parmesan before serving.

BREAKFAST BURRITO

1 PERSON

$2 / PERSON

INGREDIENTS

- 1 tortilla
- 2 eggs (scrambled)
- ¼ cup shredded cheese
- ¼ cup canned black beans
- 2 tbsp salsa

HOW TO COOK

- Layer scrambled eggs, cheese, beans, and salsa on the tortilla.
- Roll tightly into a burrito.

CAPRESE SALAD

1 PERSON

$2.5 / PERSON

INGREDIENTS

- 1 tomato (sliced)
- 4 slices fresh mozzarella
- 1 tbsp olive oil
- 1 tsp balsamic glaze
- Fresh basil leaves

HOW TO COOK

- Arrange tomato slices and mozzarella alternately on a plate.
- Drizzle with olive oil and balsamic glaze. Top with basil leaves.

SWEET AND SOUR CHICKEN

2 PEOPLE

$3 / PERSON

INGREDIENTS

- ½ lb chicken (diced)
- 1 cup pineapple chunks (canned or fresh)
- ½ cup bell peppers (diced)
- 2 tbsp soy sauce
- 2 tbsp brown sugar

HOW TO COOK

- Cook chicken in a pan until browned.
- Add pineapple, bell peppers, soy sauce, and brown sugar. Simmer until sauce thickens.

TUNA NICOISE SALAD

1 PERSON

$2.5 / PERSON

INGREDIENTS

- 1 cup mixed greens
- ½ cup canned tuna
- 1 boiled egg (sliced)
- ½ cup boiled potatoes (cubed)
- Olive oil and lemon juice (for dressing)

HOW TO COOK

- Arrange greens, tuna, egg, and potatoes on a plate.
- Drizzle with olive oil and lemon juice.

THAI PEANUT CHICKEN NOODLES

2 PEOPLE

$3 / PERSON

INGREDIENTS

- 1 cup cooked noodles
- ½ cup cooked chicken (shredded)
- 2 tbsp peanut butter
- 1 tbsp soy sauce
- 1 tsp lime juice

HOW TO COOK

- Mix peanut butter, soy sauce, and lime juice into a sauce.
- Toss noodles and chicken with the sauce.

SPINACH AND FETA STUFFED PEPPERS

2 PEOPLE

$2.5 / PERSON

INGREDIENTS

- 2 bell peppers (halved and hollowed)
- 1 cup spinach (chopped)
- ¼ cup feta cheese
- Olive oil
- Garlic

HOW TO COOK

- Sauté spinach and garlic in olive oil, then mix with feta cheese.
- Fill bell pepper halves with the mixture and bake at 375°F (190°C) for 20 minutes.

TURKEY MEATBALL SOUP

2 PEOPLE

$3 / PERSON

INGREDIENTS

- ½ lb turkey meatballs (store-bought or homemade)
- 2 cups chicken broth
- 1 cup spinach
- 1 small carrot (sliced)
- Salt and pepper

HOW TO COOK

- Heat chicken broth and add meatballs, carrots, and spinach.
- Simmer for 15 minutes and season with salt and pepper.

ZUCCHINI NOODLES WITH PESTO

1 PERSON

$2.5 / PERSON

INGREDIENTS

- 2 zucchini (spiralized or sliced into ribbons)
- 2 tbsp pesto sauce
- 1 tbsp olive oil
- Parmesan cheese
- Salt and pepper

HOW TO COOK

- Heat olive oil in a pan and sauté zucchini noodles for 2–3 minutes.
- Toss with pesto sauce and sprinkle with parmesan cheese.

BBQ PULLED CHICKEN SANDWICH

1 PERSON

$2.5 / PERSON

INGREDIENTS

- ½ cup shredded chicken
- 2 tbsp BBQ sauce
- 1 sandwich bun
- 1 tbsp mayonnaise
- Pickles (optional)

HOW TO COOK

- Mix shredded chicken with BBQ sauce.
- Spread mayonnaise on the bun and fill with the chicken mixture. Add pickles if desired.

SPINACH AND MUSHROOM OMELETTE

1 PERSON

$2 / PERSON

INGREDIENTS

- 2 eggs
- ½ cup fresh spinach
- ¼ cup sliced mushrooms
- 1 tbsp butter
- Salt and pepper

HOW TO COOK

- Sauté spinach and mushrooms in butter until tender.
- Add whisked eggs, season with salt and pepper, and cook until set.

TACO RICE BOWL

2 PEOPLE

$2.5 / PERSON

INGREDIENTS

- 1 cup cooked rice
- ½ cup ground beef or turkey
- 2 tbsp taco seasoning
- ¼ cup shredded cheese
- Salsa

HOW TO COOK

- Cook ground meat with taco seasoning.
- Serve over rice and top with cheese and salsa.

LENTIL SOUP

2 PEOPLE

$2 / PERSON

INGREDIENTS

- 1 cup dried lentils
- 2 cups vegetable broth
- 1 carrot (diced)
- 1 small onion (chopped)
- Garlic

HOW TO COOK

- Sauté onion, garlic, and carrot in a pot.
- Add lentils and broth; simmer until lentils are tender.

MEDITERRANEAN COUSCOUS SALAD

2 PEOPLE

$2.5 / PERSON

INGREDIENTS

- 1 cup cooked couscous
- ½ cup diced cucumber
- ½ cup cherry tomatoes (halved)
- ¼ cup crumbled feta cheese
- 1 tbsp olive oil

HOW TO COOK

- Mix couscous, cucumber, tomatoes, and feta in a bowl.
- Drizzle with olive oil and toss to combine.

CHICKEN STIR-FRY WITH SNAP PEAS

2 PEOPLE

$2.75 / PERSON

INGREDIENTS

- ½ cup diced chicken breast
- 1 cup snap peas
- 2 tbsp soy sauce
- 1 tsp sesame oil
- Garlic

HOW TO COOK

- Stir-fry chicken in sesame oil until cooked.
- Add snap peas, soy sauce, and garlic; cook for 2–3 minutes.

RATATOUILLE

2 PEOPLE

$2.5 / PERSON

INGREDIENTS

- 1 zucchini (sliced)
- 1 eggplant (cubed)
- ½ cup diced tomatoes
- 1 tbsp olive oil
- Garlic

HOW TO COOK

- Sauté garlic, zucchini, and eggplant in olive oil.
- Add diced tomatoes and simmer until vegetables are tender.

SHRIMP TACOS

1 PERSON

$3.25 / PERSON

INGREDIENTS

- 6–8 shrimp (peeled and deveined)
- 2 tortillas
- 1 tbsp taco seasoning
- ¼ cup shredded cabbage
- Lime wedges

HOW TO COOK

- Season shrimp with taco seasoning and cook in a pan until pink.
- Fill tortillas with shrimp, cabbage, and a squeeze of lime.

CHICKPEA WRAPS

1-2 PEOPLE

$2 / PERSON

INGREDIENTS

- 1 cup canned chickpeas
- 2 tortillas
- ¼ cup diced cucumber
- 2 tbsp hummus
- Lemon juice

HOW TO COOK

- Mash chickpeas with hummus and lemon juice.
- Spread the mixture on tortillas, then add cucumber and roll up.

VEGETABLE FRIED QUINOA

2 PEOPLE

$2.5 / PERSON

INGREDIENTS

- 1 cup cooked quinoa
- ½ cup frozen mixed vegetables
- 1 egg
- 2 tbsp soy sauce
- 1 tsp sesame oil

HOW TO COOK

- Heat sesame oil in a pan and cook the mixed vegetables.
- Add quinoa and stir-fry with soy sauce.
- Scramble the egg in the pan and mix with the quinoa.

BAKED MAC AND CHEESE

2 PEOPLE

$2.75 / PERSON

INGREDIENTS

- 1 cup pasta
- ¼ cup shredded cheese
- ¼ cup milk
- 1 tbsp butter
- Breadcrumbs

HOW TO COOK

- Cook pasta and drain.
- Mix pasta with cheese, milk, and butter, then transfer to a baking dish.
- Sprinkle breadcrumbs on top and bake at 375°F (190°C) for 10 minutes.

EGG SALAD WRAP

1 PERSON

$1.75 / PERSON

INGREDIENTS

- 2 boiled eggs
- 2 tbsp mayonnaise
- 1 tortilla
- 1 tsp mustard
- Lettuce leaves

HOW TO COOK

- Mash boiled eggs with mayonnaise and mustard.
- Spread the mixture onto a tortilla, add lettuce, and wrap tightly.

CHICKPEA AND SWEET POTATO CURRY

2 PEOPLE

$2.5 / PERSON

INGREDIENTS

- 1 sweet potato (cubed)
- 1 cup canned chickpeas
- 1 cup coconut milk
- 1 tsp curry powder
- Garlic

HOW TO COOK

- Sauté garlic, then add sweet potato and curry powder.
- Pour in coconut milk and simmer until the potato is tender.
- Stir in chickpeas and cook for 5 more minutes.

LEMON GARLIC SHRIMP PASTA

1 PERSON

$1.75 / PERSON

INGREDIENTS

- 2 boiled eggs
- 2 tbsp mayonnaise
- 1 tortilla
- 1 tsp mustard
- Lettuce leaves

HOW TO COOK

- Mash boiled eggs with mayonnaise and mustard.
- Spread the mixture onto a tortilla, add lettuce, and wrap tightly.

GREEK SALAD

1 PERSON

$2.5 / PERSON

INGREDIENTS

- 1 cup mixed greens
- ½ cup cherry tomatoes
- ¼ cup diced cucumber
- ¼ cup crumbled feta cheese
- 1 tbsp olive oil

HOW TO COOK

- Toss greens, tomatoes, cucumber, and feta cheese in a bowl.
- Drizzle with olive oil and mix.

STUFFED BELL PEPPERS WITH RICE

2 PEOPLE

$2.75 / PERSON

INGREDIENTS

- 2 bell peppers (halved and hollowed)
- 1 cup cooked rice
- ½ cup ground turkey or beef
- ½ cup marinara sauce
- Shredded cheese

HOW TO COOK

- Brown ground meat and mix with rice and marinara sauce.
- Stuff the mixture into the bell peppers and top with shredded cheese.
- Bake at 375°F (190°C) for 20 minutes.

SWEET POTATO AND BLACK BEAN TACOS

2 PEOPLE

$2.5 / PERSON

INGREDIENTS

- 1 sweet potato (cubed and roasted)
- ½ cup black beans (canned)
- 2 tortillas
- 2 tbsp salsa
- Shredded lettuce

HOW TO COOK

- Roast sweet potato cubes until tender.
- Fill tortillas with sweet potato, black beans, salsa, and lettuce.

TURKEY AND VEGGIE STIR-FRY

2 PEOPLE

$2.75 / PERSON

INGREDIENTS

- ½ cup ground turkey
- 1 cup mixed vegetables (fresh or frozen)
- 2 tbsp soy sauce
- 1 tsp sesame oil
- Garlic

HOW TO COOK

- Cook ground turkey in sesame oil until browned.
- Add mixed vegetables, soy sauce, and garlic, and stir-fry until tender.

PASTA WITH SPINACH AND RICOTTA

2 PEOPLE

$2.5 / PERSON

INGREDIENTS

- 1 cup cooked pasta
- 1 cup fresh spinach
- ¼ cup ricotta cheese
- 1 clove garlic
- Olive oil

HOW TO COOK

- Sauté garlic and spinach in olive oil until wilted.
- Toss with cooked pasta and stir in ricotta cheese.

THAT'S A WRAP!

Thank you for flipping through these recipes!

We hope this cookbook has stirred up your creativity, whisked away your hunger, and brought some zest to your kitchen adventures.

Remember, every meal you make is your own delicious masterpiece. So, keep cooking and stay saucy!

We'd also love to hear from you! If you enjoyed this cookbook, please leave a review and let us know how these recipes worked for you. Your feedback helps us serve up even more delicious ideas!

Made in the USA
Columbia, SC
29 December 2024

50858936R00048